William Blount

by Carol Ji In Lugtu

HOUGHTON MIFFLIN

BOSTON

Long Ago in Tennessee

Tennessee was not always a state. Before it became a state, it was part of North Carolina. When Tennessee became the 16th state in 1796, almost all the people who lived there lived in eastern and central Tennessee.

Many people played an important part in making Tennessee a state. One of those people was William Blount.

William Blount

Young William

William Blount was born on March 26, 1749, in northeastern North Carolina, where Bertie County is today. He was the oldest of eight children in his family.

William's father had a business that sold building supplies such as tar and turpentine. When William and his brothers were old enough, they helped their father run his business. During the American Revolution though, William left home to join the Continental Army and fight the British.

Workers gather tree sap to make turpentine.

The signing of the Constitution

North Carolina Politics

After Blount left the army, he served in North Carolina's new state government. Blount also represented North Carolina in the Continental Congress several times during the 1780s.

Blount represented North Carolina at the Constitutional Convention in 1787. He was only 38 years old. He was one of the signers of the United States Constitution.

Two years later, Blount voted for North Carolina to ratify, or approve, the Constitution.

The Southwest Territory

Before 1789, western North Carolina included all of what is now Tennessee—from the Appalachian Mountains to the Mississippi River. When North Carolina approved the U.S. Constitution in 1789, it agreed to give that land to the United States. The land was known as the Southwest Territory.

In June 1790, President George Washington appointed Blount the first governor of the Southwest Territory. Blount made Rocky Mount the capital. Rocky Mount is near present-day Johnson City, Tennessee.

As governor, Blount was appointed to the position of Superintendent of Indian Affairs. His duties included settling arguments over land between white settlers and the Cherokee.

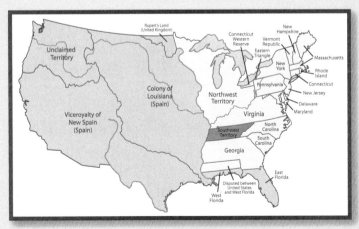

The Southwest Territory's first governor was William Blount.

James White's Fort

Settlers moving west of the Appalachian mountains were eager to own land. People already owned what little good farmland existed east of the mountains. Settlers saw Cherokee land and wanted it for themselves. When they tried to take the land, the Cherokee fought back.

In June 1791, Blount led treaty talks between settlers and the Cherokee. In July, the Cherokee and Blount signed the Treaty of Holston at James White's Fort in Knoxville. The Cherokee agreed to give up some land. This made Blount popular with the settlers, and he still got along with some Cherokee. Other Cherokee did not accept the treaty and continued to attack settlers to make them leave the territory.

Tennessee Becomes a State

Settlers in the Southwest Territory wanted to become a state. They believed that statehood would give them more protection and help them win conflicts over land with the Cherokee. In 1784, settlers in East Tennessee tried to create a new state called Franklin, named after Benjamin Franklin. The United States government, however, did not accept Franklin as a state.

In 1796, the settlers were finally successful in becoming a state. That January, Blount led a convention that wrote Tennessee's first state constitution. When the United States Congress accepted their constitution, Tennessee became a state on June 1, 1796.

Blount was elected as one of Tennessee's first United States senators that year. Two years later, he returned to Tennessee and was elected to the state senate. Blount lived in Knoxville for the rest of his life.

Tennessee's state seal

Blount Mansion

Blount's Legacy

You can still see William Blount's effect on Tennessee today. Blount Mansion, in downtown Knoxville, is a museum and National Historic Landmark. Visitors may take tours of the mansion.

The city of Maryville, in Blount County, Tennessee, is named after Blount's wife, Mary. This city is home to William Blount High School, William Blount Middle School, and Mary Blount Elementary.

William Blount played an important part in United States history. Blount tried to resolve conflicts between white settlers and Native Americans. He also guided Tennessee's entry into the United States as the 16th state.